S. Hrg. 113–104

TRANSBOUNDARY HYDROCARBON RESERVOIRS

HEARING

BEFORE THE

COMMITTEE ON
ENERGY AND NATURAL RESOURCES
UNITED STATES SENATE

ONE HUNDRED THIRTEENTH CONGRESS

FIRST SESSION

TO

CONSIDER THE FOLLOWING LEGISLATION: S. 812, A BILL TO AUTHOR-
IZE THE SECRETARY OF THE INTERIOR TO TAKE ACTIONS TO IMPLE-
MENT THE AGREEMENT BETWEEN THE UNITED STATES OF AMERICA
AND THE UNITED MEXICAN STATES CONCERNING TRANSBOUNDARY
HYDROCARBON RESERVOIRS IN THE GULF OF MEXICO; AND H.R.
1613, A BILL TO AMEND THE OUTER CONTINENTAL SHELF LANDS
ACT TO PROVIDE FOR THE PROPER FEDERAL MANAGEMENT AND
OVERSIGHT OF TRANSBOUNDARY HYDROCARBON RESERVOIRS, AND
FOR OTHER PURPOSES

OCTOBER 1, 2013

Printed for the use of the
Committee on Energy and Natural Resources

———

U.S. GOVERNMENT PRINTING OFFICE

85–407 PDF   WASHINGTON : 2013

For sale by the Superintendent of Documents, U.S. Government Printing Office
Internet: bookstore.gpo.gov   Phone: toll free (866) 512–1800; DC area (202) 512–1800
Fax: (202) 512–2104   Mail: Stop IDCC, Washington, DC 20402–0001

CONTENTS

STATEMENTS

APPENDIX

TRANSBOUNDARY HYDROCARBON RESERVOIRS

TUESDAY, OCTOBER 1, 2013

U.S. SENATE,
COMMITTEE ON ENERGY AND NATURAL RESOURCES,
Washington, DC.

The committee met, pursuant to notice, at 9:57 a.m. in room SD–366, Dirksen Senate Office Building, Hon. Ron Wyden, chairman, presiding.

OPENING STATEMENT OF HON. RON WYDEN, U.S. SENATOR FROM OREGON

The CHAIRMAN. The committee will come to order.

The purpose of today's hearing is to consider legislation to implement the U.S./Mexico Transboundary Hydrocarbon Agreement. I want to thank our witnesses, first of all, for appearing today.

For the first time in over half a century, the U.S. and Mexico are entering into a robust energy partnership between our 2 countries. Hopefully this momentum will extend to other areas of trade, investment, and mutual cooperation, renewing the North American Alliance and strengthening our economy.

The Transboundary Hydrocarbon Agreement will provide a way for the United States and Mexico to pursue the joint development of shared energy resources. This agreement resolves claims to a dispute area in the Gulf of Mexico so that the energy resources can be developed and the benefits can be shared by both Nations.

On a recent visit to Mexico, our Vice President, Vice President Biden, spoke of the need for a stronger Western Hemisphere and the special role that North America is going to play, particularly the partnership between the United States and Mexico. Vice President Biden said and I quote, "We are grounded in a common border, common culture, common values, common dreams and common potential."

In that view that's why we're here today to review legislation to implement the U.S./Mexico Transboundary Agreement.

Our country and Mexico have been working since the 1970s to provide a joint legal framework for shared resources. Such an agreement will help to grow our domestic energy supplies, ensure responsible resource management, strong environmental protection; and mutual assurance of regulatory and safety standards. I'm of the view that this agreement accomplishes that.

The agreement encourages joint development of shared reservoirs and individual development by U.S. and Mexican companies. Further, the agreement gives legal certainty to U.S. companies to explore joint ventures with Mexico's national oil company, requires joint safety inspection teams. and calls for the adoption of common safety and environmental standards.

The agreement is going to make nearly 1.5 million acres of the Western Gap of the Outer Continental Shelf available. The Bureau of Ocean Energy Management estimates that these areas could contain up to 172 million barrels of oil and 304 billion cubic feet of natural gas, making our country less dependent on foreign sources of oil and gas.

The Mexican government has acted quickly to fulfill their obligation to enact the agreement by ratifying it on April 12, 2012 and signing it into law that year. In addition to approving the agreement the Mexican government, under the leadership of President Peña Nieto, has gone a step further undertaking domestic energy reform by proposing constitutional changes for the first time since 1960. The proposed reforms would work to strengthen Mexico's energy sector by boosting investment and production.

It's the hope that through this agreement and the proposed energy reforms in Mexico that the energy revolution in the United States is now experiencing can be extended throughout the Western Hemisphere. This would make our region more competitive and less reliant on politically tumultuous States for obtaining energy.

Before concluding I'd like to take a moment to thank the Department of the Interior, the Department of State, the Mexican Embassy and all staff for diligent work and professionalism that made it possible for the committee to write S. 812 and in putting together today's hearing. The legislation that we're considering, if not signed into law before mid January, the moratorium in the Western Gap of the Gulf of Mexico expires. That could result in the damaging and loss of shared resources. That is why the committee feels it's important to move quickly.

It's also my hope that we will not only be able to quickly move, but also pass clean legislation to approve this time sensitive agreement and not get bogged down in matters that simply are not relevant to the agreement. What's important to keep in mind is the importance of the agreement and continue to work with Mexico to ensure a strong partnership and then begin the important work of integrating and creating a strong North American energy economy.

What we're going to do is Senator Murkowski has some remarks.

Senator Landrieu is on a tight schedule.

So with our witnesses? Indulgence we'll hear from Senator Murkowski and Senator Landrieu and then we're very happy to hear from our witnesses.

Senator Murkowski.

[The prepared statement of Senator Schatz follows:]

PREPARED STATEMENT OF HON. BRIAN SCHATZ, U.S. SENATOR FROM HAWAII

"Chairman Wyden and Ranking Member Murkowski, thank you for holding this hearing. This agreement between the United States and Mexico is an important one, and I am glad both the House and the Senate are moving forward to act on it.

I would like to highlight one major difference between the bills introduced by the House and the Senate. Included in the House bill, but not the Senate bill, is an exemption for U.S. oil and gas companies operating in trans-boundary areas from the requirement to disclose payments made to foreign governments for the development of oil, gas or other minerals. This requirement is also known as section 1504 of the

Dodd-Frank Act, and has strong support from transparency advocates and the White House.

I have serious concerns about this exemption, which applies to all trans-boundary areas in the world, not just the one in question today.

Other members share my reservations, and for good reason.

About two-thirds of the world's poorest people live in resource rich countries. The agreements made between these governments and companies, often extractive industries, suffer from a severe lack of transparency, which has at times enabled large-scale government corruption, and allowed companies to operate without proper public oversight.

Simple reporting requirements, as required under Section 1504 of Dodd-Frank, can help to increase transparency and decrease corruption. Including an exemption from these common-sense rules in a trans-boundary agreement such as the one before us today is unnecessary and counterproductive.

I look forward to hearing the testimonies today and hope the witnesses can shed some light on this issue."

STATEMENT OF HON. LISA MURKOWSKI, U.S. SENATOR FROM ALASKA

Senator MURKOWSKI. Thank you, Mr. Chairman and appreciate you scheduling this hearing on legislation pending before the committee to approve and implement the U.S./Mexico Transboundary Agreement.

I also want to thank our very distinguished witnesses for being here today. Look forward to the perspectives that you will share.

I view this agreement as an important step toward greater North American energy security. The Congressional Research Service says that the U.S. and Canada are "joined at the well" when it comes to energy. I believe that we should strive for the same relationship with Mexico.

Though we are strong trading partners and tied economically. More cooperation and integration is necessary to reach this goal.

Energy is already flowing between our 2 countries. Though crude oil production in Mexico continues to decline, Mexico remains one of the top exporters of crude oil to the U.S. We are Mexico's largest supplier of petroleum products. We're also sending increasing volumes of natural gas by pipeline to Mexico. So approval of the Transboundary Agreement will allow this relationship to continue and to grow.

The agreement lifts the moratorium on oil and gas leasing in the Western Gap and provides legal certainty for development along the entire Transboundary area. This will open access to over a million new acres on the Outer Continental Shelf, hundreds of millions of barrels of oil, billions of cubic feet of natural gas and lead to new jobs and new revenues.

The agreement also encourages the promotion of common safety and environmental standards though each country retains authority over activity within their respective waters.

Both of the bills authorize the Secretary of the Interior to approve unitization agreements to develop oil and gas resources in the Transboundary area, disclose information necessary to implement the agreement and manage development and to participate in and implement dispute settlements.

As the chairman has noted this agreement was signed by Mexico and the U.S. on February 20, 2012 and ratified by the Mexican Senate 2 months later. But yet more than a year later we here in the Senate have yet to do our part. It's time we act to approve the agreement and provide the Interior Department the necessary authorities to implement it.

There are some differences between the bills before us today, primarily related to scope beyond the U.S./Mexico Transboundary Agreement. So I would welcome the witnesses? thoughts on these provisions.

With that, I look forward to Senator Landrieu's comments and to hear the testimony from our witnesses.

Thank you.

The CHAIRMAN. Senator Landrieu.

STATEMENT OF HON. MARY LANDRIEU, U.S. SENATOR FROM LOUISIANA

Senator LANDRIEU. Thank you, Mr. Chairman. I really appreciate the opportunity. I've got to slip out for another meeting and then a press conference shortly on another subject.

But I wanted to be here to give my support to the concept of this legislation and to acknowledge how important it is to thank the chair and the ranking member for leading this effort to implement the Transboundary Agreement between the U.S. and Mexico. It's essential for a variety of reasons.

It will allow U.S. companies, for the first time, to partner with Mexican interest and Mexican companies to maximize production in the Gulf which will benefit not only the United States, but Mexico as well, I believe.

It will give companies the assurance they require to increase investments in deep water production near our transboundary region which is a significant area and an important area and a promising area.

The limiting factor to this point has been political, namely the lack of a working agreement on how best to manage the area claimed by both Mexico and the U.S.

Now we can understand, Mr. Chairman and ranking member, how important this is to our country. But also to the Gulf Coast which is why I'm here this morning because Louisiana is one of the 4 most producers in deep water. Many of our companies, Texas, Louisiana, are leading the effort not only in the Gulf, but around the world producing oil and gas safely in very difficult environments.

So we're very interested in this agreement.

But I want to say that one of the things that will make a difference whether I can be supportive or not is testimony today, Mr. Chairman, from our department. My question is would these lands fall under the current GOMESA, Gulf of Mexico Energy Security Act, which this committee passed which dedicates a portion of the revenues produced from this production back to the Gulf Coast States. Now that was an agreement that was reached after many years of debate in the United States. Our country said the right thing to do is to share revenues with the coastal States that serve as a production for these revenues.

So my one question, you can answer it now or submit the answer to the chairman at the appropriate time. But my vote on this bill will rest solely on the answer to that question.

If it's yes, then I will vote for the bill.

If it's no, I will not be able to because we have set a very strong policy in the Gulf of Mexico on the U.S. side of this border that we believe that it is fair as a Nation. I would hope Mexico would look at our model and maybe adopt it. That it's fair to share the revenues, not just with the Federal Government of Mexico and the United States, but with the States that serve as host to the production.

Some of that production is done in Alaska, not in this situation, but Alaska and their coastal communities should benefit from that production and share with all the taxpayers of the country, but also with the coastal communities. That agreement has been in place for interior States since 1920, that sharing of revenues.

So Mr. Beaudreau, should he answer that now or later, Mr. Chairman?

The CHAIRMAN. Let's do this.

First of all the Senator from Louisiana knows I'm going to work very closely with her on all these matters.

Let's do this. Let's have the witnesses make their statements. But I would like it to be stated now for the record that my first question is Senator Landrieu's question, so that we will begin questioning, when I'm recognized for purposes of that, to have an answer to Senator Landrieu's question.

Is that acceptable?

Senator LANDRIEU. That is very acceptable. Thank you for your graciousness.

The CHAIRMAN. We'll be working together.

Alright. Gentlemen, welcome.

The Honorable Carlos Pascual and the Honorable Tommy Beaudreau and we'll have your statements and you all know what my first question will be. So you have a little time to prepare for my first question as well.

Let's begin with you, Mr. Pascual. We thank you for the cooperation, of course, that the State Department has shown.

Welcome.

STATEMENT OF CARLOS PASCUAL, SPECIAL ENVOY AND CO-ORDINATOR, INTERNATIONAL ENERGY AFFAIRS, DEPART-MENT OF STATE

Mr. PASCUAL. Thank you very much, Chairman Wyden and Ranking Member Murkowski and Senator Landrieu as well for participating in your sponsorship. These were excellent opening statements that you made. I couldn't agree more with the way that you framed the issue. Thank you for putting it in that extremely constructive context and the opportunity to reinforce the statements that you've already made.

The issues of energy security have been paramount concerns of the State Department and of concerns for Secretary Kerry. They obviously are for these committees. It's very appropriate that you've put this whole issue in the context of energy security because in the end that's fundamentally what we're trying to support for the United States, a more secure energy future.

The Administration supports the swift passage of legislation to allow for the implementation of the Transboundary Agreement signed by Mexico and the United States, as you've indicated, in

February 2012. As you've indicated it was ratified by Mexico in April 2012.

So the positive thing is that with passage of legislation here we are ready to move. What this would do is it could allow Mexico and the United States to move immediately, to bring immediate, the agreement into full force and facilitate cooperation between U.S. companies and Mexico's national oil company, PEMEX, to develop resources that would strengthen North America's potential role as a hub for energy security.

Let me begin by stressing the importance that the State Department assigns to a strong energy partnership with Mexico, as you have said, Senator Wyden.

Our energy trading relationship with Mexico is essential to securing stable flows to the United States' markets. That is critical to sustained U.S. economic growth.

In fact in 2012 energy related trade with Mexico totaled $65 billion. Mexico has, as was indicated, 10.2 billion barrels in proven reserves. But its production has fallen by more than 30 percent from 2004 to 2012.

Still a more positive future for Mexican production is very much within reach.

Mexican President Enrique Peña Nieto is making reform a priority. His party submitted legislation for comprehensive energy reform in August. With passage of the reform Mexico could attract international investment to develop its hydrocarbon resources and reverse the decline in oil production. The implementation of the Transboundary Agreement could provide a down payment on those prospects for investment.

The agreement itself would establish a framework that would allow for the development of hydrocarbon reservoirs that cross the maritime boundary with Mexico.

It would provide the legal certainty companies need to invest in reservoirs along our maritime boundary. This would allow U.S. companies to invest in lease blocks along the boundary and where appropriate, jointly explore and develop reservoirs in the boundary area with Mexico as units. The benefits of managing a reservoir as a single unit, long standing practice in the U.S. side of the Gulf, are well developed and well known.

The agreement would extend these benefits to the management of transboundary reserves allowing U.S. companies to partner with PEMEX to minimize drilling, maximize recovery and achieve the environmental benefits that arise from drilling fewer wells.

Even as the agreement opens more acreage to drilling it would do so in a responsible way. Mexico is already moving into the deep water regions of the Gulf along our maritime boundary. We can either drill competitively or we can work collaboratively.

With the passage of the legislation, an entry in force of the agreement, we would put in place a framework to not only minimize the number of wells drilled along the boundary. But to provide for joint safety and environmental inspections on all activity that takes place under the agreement.

Both sides would gain from reciprocal arrangements.

Mexico would still apply and enforce laws in its jurisdiction.

We would still apply and enforce laws in ours.

But the agreement would allow U.S. inspectors to join Mexican inspectors on their rigs and vice versa.

In addition we would work together to review regulations to make sure that each side has an appropriate framework.

We would review and approve all activity under the agreement whether it occurs in areas under Mexican jurisdiction or under ours giving us the ability to ensure that reservoirs along our boundary conform to appropriate safety standards.

This is a business friendly arrangement that will potentially increase revenues and energy security. It comes with strong safety and environmental provisions.

We welcome S. 812 in the interest of both the Senate and the House in passing legislation providing congressional approval of and granting the Secretary of the Interior the authority to implement the Transboundary Agreement. Our continued engagement and progress is a promising step forward to implementing the U.S./Mexico Transboundary Agreement.

As noted in the statement of Administration policy on H.R. 1613, we support passage of legislation focused specifically on the agreement without the inclusion of provisions such as those related to section 1504 of the Dodd-Frank Act that would directly delude U.S. efforts to increase transparency and accountability.

We look forward to working with the Department of the Interior and the committee on expeditious approval of this important piece of legislation.

In conclusion, we are encouraged by the accelerating pace of movement on finalizing this agreement. As many congressional members have stated, it is a win/win for the United States and Mexico.

I appreciate the time you are devoting to this issue. Hope that we have addressed your request for information on many potential benefits for both the United States and Mexico. We look forward to answering your specific questions. Thank you for giving us, Assistant Secretary Beaudreau and myself, the opportunity to appear before you.

[The prepared statement of Mr. Pascual follows:]

PREPARED STATEMENT OF CARLOS PASCUAL, SPECIAL ENVOY AND COORDINATOR, INTERNATION ENERGY AFAIRS, DEPARTMENT OF STATE

Chairman Wyden, Ranking Member Murkowski, and other Members of the Committee on Energy and Natural Resources, I appreciate the opportunity to appear before you today.

I know that each and every Member of this Committee is concerned about our nation's energy security, and I can assure you that Secretary Kerry and the Department of State share that concern. For that reason, I am happy to be here today to discuss the Transboundary Agreement between Mexico and the United States. The Administration supports the swift passage of legislation to allow for the implementation of the Transboundary Agreement signed by Mexico and the United States on February 20, 2012 and we appreciate the Chair and Ranking Member for their leadership in introducing legislation. We look forward to working with Congress on Senate Bill 812 to accelerate the safe and effective development of hydrocarbon resources that cross the maritime boundary between Mexico and the United States in the Gulf of Mexico.

Let me begin by stressing the importance that the State Department assigns to fostering a stable energy partnership with Mexico. Our energy trading relationship with Mexico is an important component of North American energy security. Mexico is our third largest supplier of imported crude oil and the largest export market for U.S. refined petroleum products; in fact, energy-related trade with Mexico totaled

$65 billion in 2012. Mexico is also a growing market for U.S. natural gas exports. By establishing greater legal clarity for the development of reserves that traverse the U.S.-Mexico maritime boundary in the Gulf of Mexico, the Transboundary Agreement would bring significant benefits to the United States and Mexico.

The United States and Canada have experienced an increase in energy production as a result of private investment, entrepreneurial ingenuity, technological innovation and strong commodity prices. In 2012, domestic oil production climbed to the highest level in 15 years. In contrast, Mexico has 10.2 billion barrels in proven reserves, but its production fell by over one third from 2004 to 2012, and projections forecast Mexican production will continue to decline in the short-term. This significant trend is often attributed to the maturation of major fields and the challenges for the national oil company, Petroeos Mexicanos (PEMEX), to maintain the necessary levels of investment in the sector.

Mexican President Pena Nieto has made energy reform a priority. His party submitted legislation for comprehensive energy reform in August 2013 and, with passage of the reform, Mexico could attract international investment and expertise to help develop its hydrocarbon resources and reverse the decline in oil production. The Transboundary Agreement could be a down payment on the promise of more fundamental reform. With entry into force of the Agreement, companies would have a framework to develop resources crossing the U.S. maritime boundary with Mexico as the current lack of a framework renders these resources too risky to tap. The projects that would be enabled by the Agreement would demonstrate that cooperation between PEMEX and international oil companies, including those based in the U.S., has the potential to produce significant resources and revenues to benefit the Mexican people and economy.

Despite the challenges facing Mexico in the near term, the exciting story here is that North American energy production as a whole could boost our respective national and global energy security. North American energy resources provide the prospect not only of assuring our own energy supply, but of contributing to global market supplies and helping promote the stability in global energy markets that we need to support our domestic economic growth. Such opportunities, including the Transboundary Agreement between the United States and Mexico, could support increased Mexican and North American production capacity and could be critical to world supplies and economic growth.

Background

The Transboundary Agreement between the United States and Mexico addresses the development of oil and gas reservoirs that cross the maritime boundary between our two countries in the Gulf of Mexico (excluding submerged lands under Texas jurisdiction). The Mexican Senate overwhelmingly approved the Agreement in April 2012. The Administration previously proposed legislative language that would provide the Secretary of the Interior the necessary authority to implement the Agreement. S. 812 closely resembles this language, and its passage would allow implementation to commence quickly.

Role of the Agreement

The Transboundary Agreement is an important step in our national efforts to secure our energy future and, at the same time, promote a stronger and long-term cooperative relationship with Mexico in meeting each country's energy security goals. We believe the agreement would help facilitate the safe and responsible management of offshore petroleum reservoirs that straddle our maritime boundary and strengthen overall our bilateral relations.

The Agreement would enable meaningful energy sector collaboration between the United States and Mexico (and in particular between U.S. operators and PEMEX), which we believe would provide U.S. operators the opportunity to demonstrate the benefits of their participation in the Mexican energy market, potentially leading to deeper and more meaningful collaboration over time.

This Agreement will make nearly 1.5 million acres of the Outer Continental Shelf more attractive to U.S. operators by unlocking areas for exploration and development along our maritime boundary within U.S. jurisdiction . The Agreement would eliminate the moratorium on drilling along the boundary in the Western Gap, and provide legal certainty needed for investment in the boundary region. It would allow American companies to enter into unitization agreements with PEMEX for the joint exploration and development of resources in the areas covered by the Agreement. The development of a reservoir as a single unit allows companies to agree how to manage the reservoir jointly in the most efficient manner, generally reducing the amount of required drilling and therefore reducing environmental impact. Each unitization agreement would be required to comply with applicable safety standards.

As a package, these arrangements could increase revenues and provide greater energy security, while mitigating safety and environmental risks that could result from unilateral development along the boundary.

We are pleased that the Agreement would advance safety and environmental protection in the Gulf. First, it provides for a system of joint inspections for all activity that takes place under the agreement. Though Mexican law would apply to operations under Mexican jurisdiction and U.S. law would apply to operations under U.S. jurisdiction, each side would have the ability to work with the other to ensure that all activity that takes place under the Agreement—wherever it occurs-meets all applicable laws and standards. In addition, under the Agreement our two countries would continue to work together to ensure that our respective standards and requirements are compatible where appropriate for the safe, effective, and environmentally responsible implementation of the Agreement.

In all aspects, the Transboundary Agreement offers the United States and Mexico significant benefits. It would, for the first time, establish a framework that would facilitate the development of hydrocarbon reservoirs that cross our maritime boundary with Mexico. This is a business friendly arrangement with strong safety and environmental provisions.

S. 812-H.R. 1613

We welcome S.812 and the interest of both the Senate and the House in passing legislation providing the Secretary of the Interior the authority to implement the Transboundary Agreement. As noted in the Statement of Administration Policy on H.R. 1613, we support passage of legislation focused specifically on the Agreement, without the inclusion of provisions such as those relating to Section 1504 of the Dodd-Frank Act that would directly dilute U.S. efforts to increase transparency and accountability. We look forward to working with the Department of the Interior and the Committee on expeditious approval of this important piece of legislation.

Conclusion

In conclusion, we are encouraged by the accelerating pace of interest and movement on implementing this agreement, which provides a much needed mechanism to facilitate the responsible and efficient exploration and development of hydrocarbon resources along the U.S.-Mexico maritime boundary. As many Congressional Members have stated, it is a "win-win" for the United States and Mexico and a win for North American energy security because it fosters stronger relationships in the development of our shared energy resources.

I appreciate the time you and your staff are devoting to this issue and hope that we addressed to your satisfaction your requests for information on the many potential benefits for both the United States and Mexico, should the Agreement be brought into force.

Thank you again for this opportunity to testify before this Subcommittee and I would be pleased to answer any questions the subcommittee might have.

The CHAIRMAN. Very helpful and again, commendations for the good work of all the folks at State who have been on this.

Mr. Beaudreau, welcome.

STATEMENT OF TOMMY P. BEAUDREAU, ACTING ASSISTANT SECRETARY, LAND AND MINERALS MANAGEMENT, DEPARTMENT OF THE INTERIOR

Mr. BEAUDREAU. Good morning, Chairman Wyden, Ranking Member Murkowski. I'm pleased to appear before you today to discuss legislation to implement the agreement between the United States of America and the United Mexican States concerning transboundary hydrocarbon reservoirs in the Gulf of Mexico. I'm also very pleased to appear this morning before the committee alongside Ambassador Pascual, who is one of the Nation's foremost experts in diplomats with respect to our relationship with Mexico as well as global energy issues.

I'd like to begin my testimony today by highlighting a couple of central points about the benefits to the United States and to the U.S. industry that implementation of the U.S./Mexico Transboundary Reservoir Agreement offers.

Offshore oil and gas development in the Gulf of Mexico has been and will remain one of the cornerstones of the United States' energy portfolio. The offshore oil and gas industry continues to invest tremendous amounts of capital and know how into exploring and developing oil and gas resources in the Gulf. This includes spurring the technical innovations necessary to safely and responsibly develop emerging, world class prospects in deep and ultra deep water.

During BOEM's offshore oil and gas lease sales in the Gulf of Mexico over the last 2 years industry has invested more than $3 billion in leases, the bulk of which was directed toward promising emerging prospects in the deep water. Despite industry's general enthusiasm for exploration and development in the deep water Gulf of Mexico, leasing in the vicinity of the U.S./Mexico maritime boundary has been muted. Areas in U.S. waters within 1.4 miles of the maritime boundary currently are under moratorium and cannot be leased.

More broadly, however, the entire Western Gap boundary region is currently subject to legal uncertainty about how potential transboundary reservoirs would be handled. Therefore, in my view, industry has been reluctant to move aggressively into those areas.

For example, there are currently 379 unleased blocks in the Western and Central Gulf near the maritime boundary and only 14 of those blocks have been leased.

Implementation of the Transboundary Reservoir Agreement would provide this much needed legal certainty to the region and is in alignment with our goals to promote safe and responsible development of our Nation's offshore oil and gas resources.

The agreement also is, I believe, strongly supported by industry. It is a pragmatic agreement designed to encourage voluntary, commercial solutions between companies operating on the U.S. side of the maritime boundary and their counterpart PEMEX on the Mexican side. We worked with U.S. industry during the negotiation of the agreement to ensure that the agreement, not only provide the legal certainty necessary to justify investment in this region, but also would be commercially workable.

The central principle of the agreement is to encourage voluntary unitization agreements between U.S. side companies and PEMEX to equitably allocate production from any reservoir spanning the maritime boundary. Unitization is a very familiar concept that is applied daily by companies working in the U.S. Gulf of Mexico. Ultimately if no voluntary unitization agreement can be reached the company would be able to move forward with development unilaterally.

Finally, the Transboundary Reservoir Agreement represents an important step in promoting safe and responsible development in a technically challenging operating environment on both sides of the boundary. Under the heightened standards that followed from Deepwater Horizon, U.S. industry is working more safely and responsibly than ever before. This agreement would not only—would not change U.S. laws or regulations that industry works under, but does provide further opportunity for cooperation between the United States and Mexico to promote high standards for safety and environmental protection applicable to all companies working in and near U.S. waters.

I appreciate, very much, S. 812 introduced in April by this committee to implement the Transboundary Agreement. We support this legislation and look forward to continuing to work with Congress to improve this important agreement.

Thank you.

[The prepared statement of Mr. Beaudreau follows:]

PREPARED STATEMENT OF TOMMY P. BEAUDREAU, ACTING ASSISTANT SECRETARY, LAND AND MINERALS MANAGEMENT, DEPARTMENT OF THE INTERIOR

Chairman Wyden, Ranking Member Murkowski, and members of the Committee, I am pleased to appear before you today to discuss legislation to implement the Agreement between the United States of America and the United Mexican States Concerning Transboundary Hydrocarbon Reservoirs in the Gulf of Mexico.

Background

On February 20, 2012, the United States and Mexico signed an Agreement concerning the development of oil and gas reservoirs that cross the international maritime boundary between the two countries in the Gulf of Mexico (excluding submerged lands under Texas jurisdiction). This Agreement would establish a framework for the cooperative exploration and development of these hydrocarbon resources. The Mexican Senate overwhelmingly approved the Agreement in April 2012. The Administration wants to work with Congress to ensure implementing legislation approving the Agreement and providing the necessary authority to bring it into force is passed. The administration appreciates the work done by Chairman Wyden and Ranking Member Murkowski to introduce S. 812, legislation that provides for such authority, and we support its swift passage. As the Administration has previously stated, we do not support the extraneous provisions included in H.R. 1613, The Outer Continental Shelf Transboundary Hydrocarbon Agreements Authorization Act as passed in the House of Representatives.

The Agreement would allow, for the first time, leaseholders on the U.S. side of the maritime boundary to cooperate with the Mexican national oil company, Petróleos Mexicanos (PEMEX), in the joint exploration and safe and responsible development of hydrocarbon resources. This agreement will make nearly 1.5 million acres of the Outer Continental Shelf, currently affected by a moratorium under the Western Gap Treaty, immediately available for leasing and also make the entire transboundary region, which is currently subject to legal uncertainty in the absence of an agreement, more attractive to U.S.-qualified operators. For example, the Department of the Interior's Bureau of Ocean Energy Management estimates that the transboundary area contains as much as 172 million barrels of oil and 304 billion cubic feet of natural gas.

Benefits of Implementing the Agreement

The Agreement provides a legal framework for cooperative offshore oil and gas development along the maritime boundary, sets clear guidelines and provides legal certainty for those operations, supports the President's goal of ensuring domestic energy security and demonstrates our shared duty to exercise responsible stewardship of the natural resources in the Gulf of Mexico. It is built on a commitment to the safe, efficient, environmentally sound, and equitable development of transboundary reservoirs. The Agreement also offers the potential for generating additional revenue for the United States and Gulf States from the lease blocks located along the delimited U.S.-Mexico maritime boundary in the Gulf of Mexico.

The Mexican market has long been closed to participation by U.S. companies, but a 2008 energy reform law in Mexico opened a window for joint hydrocarbon exploration and development with foreign entities as long as it would take place pursuant to an international agreement on transboundary reservoirs. The Agreement would take advantage of that opening. It would also end the moratorium on development along the boundary in the Western Gap and provide U.S.-qualified leaseholders with legal certainty regarding the development of transboundary reservoirs along the entire boundary so as to encourage investment. The Agreement would remove legal and structural barriers that currently impede exploration and safe and responsible development along our maritime boundary with Mexico. A significant portion of the U.S. maritime boundary with Mexico—the full length of the boundary in the Western Gap—is affected by a moratorium on drilling and exploration pursuant to the Western Gap Treaty. Upon entry into force the Agreement would lift the moratorium and open up this area—nearly ten percent of the U.S. portion of the Gap—to hydrocarbon development. Finally, having the Agreement in place will mitigate the safety and environmental risks that would result from unilateral exploration and development along the boundary.

Implementing Legislation

The implementing legislation would provide the necessary domestic legal authority to implement certain key terms of the Agreement, including:

- To authorize the Secretary of the Interior to approve unitization agreements and other arrangements necessary for the management of the transboundary reservoirs and geologic structures subject to the Agreement;
- To make available, in certain narrow circumstances necessary for the functioning of the Agreement, information related to the exploration, safe and responsible development, and production of a transboundary reservoir that may be considered confidential, privileged, or proprietary under law; and
- To participate in the Agreement's dispute resolution processes.

One of the fundamental components of the Agreement would allow leaseholders on the U.S. side of the boundary and PEMEX to explore and develop jointly as a "unit" a transboundary reservoir or geologic structure, as leaseholders frequently do on the U.S. side of the boundary. The Agreement is designed to provide incentives for PEMEX and U.S.-qualified operators to enter into voluntary unitization agreements governing the development of transboundary reservoirs. Unitization—where two or more leaseholders manage the exploration and development of a resource as a unit through a single operator—promotes the rational, efficient production of a resource, reduces waste, and minimizes the number of wells that must be drilled. Existing leases are not covered by the Agreement; however, existing lessees may voluntarily opt-in to the framework if they so choose.

In cases where a unitization agreement is not initially reached between a U.S.-qualified operator and PEMEX, the Agreement provides a process to determine whether the reservoir in question is, in fact, a transboundary reservoir that should come under the Agreement, and a carefully-calibrated process to determine the allocation of the resource between the two countries and provide the U.S. operator and PEMEX another opportunity to form a unitization agreement. If they cannot reach an agreement, the Agreement would ultimately allow for unilateral production by each side, up to the amount of hydrocarbons that exists on its side of the boundary. In other words, in these circumstances U.S.-qualified operators and PEMEX would individually develop the resources on each side of the border while protecting each nation's interests, resources and sovereignty. We anticipate, however, that the same economic incentives that currently drive voluntary unitization offshore the U.S. will similarly drive voluntary unitization under the Agreement, and that this mechanism will be rarely if ever used.

The Agreement encourages the United States and Mexico to promote common safety and environmental standards. However, the U.S. is under no obligation to alter its existing environmental laws or standards. Mexico's standards will apply to operations under Mexican jurisdiction and U.S. standards will apply to operations under U.S. jurisdiction.

The Agreement would also establish a system of joint inspections, which would allow U.S. safety personnel to inspect PEMEX facilities involved in a transboundary operation. Again, however, each jurisdiction retains its authority and responsibility to regulate activity on its side of the boundary. The DOI's Bureau of Safety and Environmental Enforcement and the United States Coast Guard already maintain a strong working relationship with the Mexican offshore regulatory authority, the Comisión Nacional Hidrocarburos (CNH), and this Agreement promotes further cooperation between the U.S. and Mexico with respect to drilling safety and oil spill response standards and practices.

S. 812

S. 812 introduced on April 25, 2013, authorizes the Secretary of the Interior to take actions to implement the Agreement between the United States of America and the United Mexican States Concerning Transboundary Hydrocarbon Reservoirs in the Gulf of Mexico. We appreciate the opportunity to provide the following preliminary views at this time.

Generally, the bill would authorize the Secretary to approve unitization agreements and related arrangements for the exploration of, and development or production of oil or gas from, transboundary reservoirs and geological structures; to disclose as necessary under the Agreement information related to the exploration, development, and production of a transboundary reservoir or geological structure that may be considered confidential, privileged, or proprietary information under law;

and to accept and take action not inconsistent with an expert determination under the Agreement.

We support this legislation and the Administration welcomes the opportunity to work with Congress to approve this important agreement.

Conclusion

In sum, the Agreement provides a much needed mechanism to facilitate the responsible and efficient exploration and development of hydrocarbon resources along the U.S. Mexico maritime boundary and provides new opportunities for U.S. companies. The Agreement provides incentives for PEMEX and U.S.-qualified operators to enter into voluntary commercial agreements to unitize transboundary reservoirs and does not change the application of existing laws or alter existing standards. Once the Agreement is in force, both the Bureau of Ocean Energy Management and the Bureau of Safety and Environmental Enforcement will assume their respective regulatory responsibilities to implement the Agreement as authorized.

Mr. Chairman, we look forward to working with the committee to enact legislation implementing this important Agreement with our Mexican partners in Gulf of Mexico energy development.

The CHAIRMAN. Thank you very much, Mr. Beaudreau.

The question that I indicated I would ask first is Senator Landrieu's. So let's note that for the record.

The question to restate it in terms of Senator Landrieu's concern is do the lands affected by the U.S./Mexico Transboundary Agreement fall under the Gulf of Mexico Energy Security Act, known as GOMESA, for purposes of revenue sharing?

Mr. BEAUDREAU. Yes. Any production——

The CHAIRMAN. The answer is yes?

Mr. BEAUDREAU. Yes. Any production coming from these areas would be covered under existing royalty sharing arrangements with the States. I think quite wisely the legislation doesn't attempt to modify the royalty sharing program in any respect.

I understand there's ongoing discussions about whether it would be appropriate to modify royalty sharing relative to the State. We're happy to continue participating in those discussions as they move forward.

The CHAIRMAN. OK.

Ambassador Pascual, in my opening statement I spoke of an emerging energy economy. The United States and Mexico are embarking on an agreement that provides an opportunity for our partnership to continue to grow and extend to other areas of commerce and trade.

I am interested in hearing from you regarding any thoughts that you may have with respect to what would be the consequences if the Congress does not move quickly to implement the agreement. What are the consequences and what might be the effects, not just in terms of energy, but in terms of our overall dialog between the United States and Mexico in the effort to create more jobs?

Mr. PASCUAL. Senator, thank you for focusing attention on that question.

I think the first issue is to look at the positive side of it, of what the potential would be because that helps us understand the consequences.

North America is going through an energy revolution. We've gone through it in the United States where we've increased oil production by more than 30 percent in 5 years, gas production by 25 percent in the last 5 years. Canada has major increases in both oil and gas production. Mexico has gone in the other direction.

Mexico has recognized that what it needs to do is to create the incentives to bring in private investment. That's one of the reasons that they've passed or have proposed a major energy reform which is under consideration right now.

So the intent, the objective is to be able to create a hub in North America for energy security which is going to be beneficial for the United States in terms of its access to energy resources, but also as a stabilizing force in global markets. The Transboundary Agreement is the first down payment of the potential that we could see between, in cooperation between the United States and Mexico. That cooperation in the past was previously prohibited by law.

By having this Transboundary Agreement it allows, in the interim, the ability to create a framework where American companies and Mexican companies can begin to work together to demonstrate the impact that those American companies can have on greater productivity in transboundary areas. In doing that we set the foundation for something which is even bigger that can come, how North America together, and Mexico and the United States, can be a foundation for energy supplies that are going to be beneficial to our supplies at home and increase our competitiveness by having even more access to natural gas at prices that are affordable and are lower than what we've seen in other parts of the world.

So this is a huge opportunity to be able to advance competitiveness. It's a huge opportunity to demonstrate that American investments in international investment is a tool to productivity and that it can be done in a way that retains the confidence of Mexican industry and the Mexican people.

The CHAIRMAN. Mr. Beaudreau, a question for you, again, about the consequences of inaction.

We heard testimony with respect to efforts with the United States and Mexico in terms of resource management, the safety inspection teams moving to adopt common safety and environmental standards. What's the result of Congressional inaction in terms of safety and environmental oversight if this does not go forward?

Mr. BEAUDREAU. Thank you for that.

Following the spill we, at the Interior Department through BOEM and BSEE redoubled our efforts to support the fledgling oil and gas regulator in Mexico, CNH, their national hydrocarbon commission. As everyone here appreciates a spill in the Gulf of Mexico will not respect the boundaries of the Nation that authorized the drilling activity. So it only makes sense that we have a common approach to safety and to our ability to respond in the event of an accident.

We will continue working with CNH to provide support regardless of whether there's an agreement. But frankly, having this agreement in place, having formal relationships between U.S. operators and PEMEX, relative to these areas, goes very far in supporting and strengthening those relationships both with PEMEX and with CNH. So it would be a major lost opportunity if we were to let this go by.

The CHAIRMAN. Very good.

Senator Murkowski.

Senator MURKOWSKI. Thank you, Mr. Chairman.

Gentlemen, thank you for your testimony this morning.

Ambassador Pascual, you mentioned the benefits to North American energy independence, energy security, all of which I absolutely agree with. You've also referred to or you've outlined it this way that we can either drill competitively or collaboratively and focus jointly on the environmental considerations, the safety considerations, looking at this agreement that we have in front of us. I certainly view it as an opportunity, a positive opportunity, on a lot of different fronts.

The Chairman has asked you a little bit about, you know, the benefits then that flow from this. I'd ask you to speak to what the downside is, again, if we fail to advance this Transboundary Agreement and more from the diplomatic perspective. You've mentioned that this is kind of a down payment on a relationship with Mexico and helping them in other ways.

But we're dealing with the situation with our neighbors on our northern border, with Canada. We're trying to figure out how we would be able to advance a Keystone XL pipeline. I look at this on the southern side and would suggest that it's important that we have good relationships, good diplomatic relationships, with our neighbors.

I guess I would ask you to detail what you think the response would be if the United States fails to engage on this Transboundary Agreement before such time, before the end of the year here. It's been noted that Mexico has already acted. We have been sitting on it now for a year.

How will we be viewed by our neighbors to the south if we fail to act?

Mr. PASCUAL. There we go.

Thank you, Senator for putting it so sharply and in focus.

The issues of hydrocarbons development have been hugely sensitive in Mexico since 1938 with the nationalization of oil. After that period of time the ability for Mexico to cooperate with any outside entity on the development of hydrocarbon resources has been virtually non-existent, except for some form of service contracts.

Mexico took on, as a matter of good faith, that because of the transboundary nature of these reserves that it should find a way to work together with the United States in the development of these resources. It was, what some might consider, I think, a courageous political act because of the sensitivity of these issues.

For Mexico it took on in good faith the willingness to pass this, recognizing that the United States was going to take longer in moving forward. It has been a long period of time.

There's a risk that if we do not pass this before the moratorium that it would be seen that the United States has reneged on a commitment to cooperate on the development of international energy resources. That will not only have a negative impact on the seriousness and the commitment of the United States, but particularly in an area that has been one of tremendous sensitivity.

The timing, in many ways, is also particularly critical because of Mexico's energy reform. In that energy reform that President Peña Nieto has proposed, Mexico would since 1938 for the first time allow for the development of private contracts with international companies that would foresee the possibility of joint ventures between American companies and PEMEX. So at the very time that

Mexico is looking at the potential for much deeper reform the United States would be sending a message that on the areas that we have agreed to cooperate and follow up that we have pulled back and reneged.

That's not only negative to our diplomatic relationship. Frankly it's negative for American companies that eventually will have a significant interest in investment in Mexican energy resources. If one looks at developments in the Gulf of Mexico, if you look at a map that is shot from overhead, the U.S. side of the border is filled with investment opportunities. The south of that is almost blank.

It's not because the resources aren't there. It's because the conditions haven't been there. The opportunities may finally be created where those resources could actually be exploited.

So from both the diplomatic perspective and a commercial perspective, not to move forward is sending exactly the wrong signal to Mexico at a critical time when we have real positive opportunity since 1938 to demonstrate the cooperation with American companies on the development of hydrocarbons resources is good for Mexico's economy, good for the Mexican people and can be done in a way that's environmentally sound.

Senator MURKOWSKI. Thank you. I appreciate the very thorough explanation. I think it's important to have all of that out on the record.

Mr. Beaudreau, you mentioned the fact that the unitization agreements are voluntary. What happens if there is no unitization agreement that can be reached?

Now you have suggested that you—a lessee could move forward unilaterally. How would that actually operate? How long do you try to work something out until such time as somebody decides that they might be able to move unilaterally?

Mr. BEAUDREAU. The entire agreement, as I mentioned in my opening statement, really takes a pragmatic approach to encourage voluntary unitization between a U.S. side operator and PEMEX and provides time in which to do that. So at the first stage—there's phases under the agreement.

At the first stage the companies have about 6 months to see if they can, without any encouragement from the outside, work out an agreement. Frankly the U.S. industry has already begun working on model unitization agreements that could be used.

If that's not successful the companies have an opportunity to bring an outside expert, a third party expert, to help resolve any technical issues around the reservoir.

In total neither side can move forward with the Transboundary Reservoir, bring it into production for a 16 month period.

If after 16 months no voluntary unitization agreement can be reached the operator would be allowed to move forward unilaterally.

All that said, we believe and I think industry believes there are such strong commercial incentives to do this. This is why there hasn't been unilateral development in the area already. There's such strong incentives to have an agreement for orderly development that we actually think cases of unilateral development would be pretty rare.

Senator MURKOWSKI. I've just got one more quick question.

The CHAIRMAN. Yes, sure.

Senator MURKOWSKI. If I may, Mr. Chairman.

The CHAIRMAN. Of course.

Senator MURKOWSKI. Should the Transboundary Agreement be approved and the legislation to implement it be approved, does the Department have plans to hold any lease sales within the Transboundary area?

Mr. BEAUDREAU. Yes.

In fact in our recent sales we have annual sales in both the Western and Central Gulf. Both planning areas implicate this transboundary area. Up until now we have offered those areas, interest in the areas have been muted because of the uncertainty.

We've also held any bids that we've received in those areas. There have been a few, not many. There have been a few.

We've held those bids with the understanding with the bidder that unless the agreement is put into effect, we wouldn't award the leases. This removes all of that uncertainty and would allow us not only to receive bids, but make the awards as well.

Senator MURKOWSKI. So just so that I understand that.

If—assuming that this agreement is put in place. We've got the legislation to implement it. You would already have interested applicants for those lease sales that have been received prior to that time of implementation.

So you would act on those. Then there would be subsequent lease sales following that?

Mr. BEAUDREAU. No. We would be able to offer those—there are companies interested in the area.

Senator MURKOWSKI. Right.

Mr. BEAUDREAU. Assuming this uncertainty can be removed.

We would continue to offer the areas, but be in a better position to actually award the leases.

Senator MURKOWSKI. OK.

Mr. BEAUDREAU. So these areas in the Central Gulf would be offered in our upcoming sale next spring, for example.

Senator MURKOWSKI. So these have already been identified in terms of where they are and in the interest shown them?

Mr. BEAUDREAU. Correct.

Senator MURKOWSKI. OK. Great.

I appreciate that clarification.

Thank you, Mr. Chairman.

The CHAIRMAN. Senator Manchin.

Senator MANCHIN. Thank you, Chairman and Senator Murkowski.

You know I stated many times before achieving energy independence is the most critical thing we can do as a country. I've felt that way. I come from a little State of West Virginia, who is a tremendous energy producer and has contributed quite a bit and wants to continue to contribute.

Working with our neighbors, North American neighbors, we think is essential to achieving this priority. I've continued to support an all in energy policy which basically would be in consideration of the XL pipeline, Keystone XL pipeline, which I wholeheartedly support. I think that anything we can do to develop what we have here in North America is going to be great for all of us.

We know there's significant oil and natural gas reserves in the areas covered by these bills that we're talking about. Developing the reserves would not only reduce our energy dependence on countries outside of North America, but it will also create good paying jobs which is a win/win for our country right now. So we appreciate this opportunity that we can find some common ground that we can move forward.

What I would like to ask, I think, is that to the Ambassador.

How do you see the agreement affecting the North America's role in the global energy market and I mean an entire market making us less dependent, be more secure? Do you believe that that can happen? This is something that we should be moving forward on?

Mr. PASCUAL. Senator, yes, absolutely. Indeed both Senator Wyden and Senator Murkowski have been reinforcing this point. I've been trying to reinforce it as well. We agree with you completely on the importance of trying to bring forward the North American energy resources that can help reinforce Americans, North Americans self reliance.

I think a couple of critical factors to put into account, to take into account, is that the United States already has vastly increased its energy production, as you well know, coming from a heavy energy producing State both in oil and gas.

Canada is increasing its production of oil and gas. Mexico has gone in the opposite direction.

One of the things that Mexico needs in order to be able to join that more North American trend is the kind of technology and investment that's necessary, particularly in deep water and unconventional oil and gas development.

So for that reason Mexico has undertaken a couple of initiatives.

One is this Transboundary Agreement because it recognizes that for transboundary reserves it needs cooperation between PEMEX, the Mexican oil company and international companies, U.S. companies, to be able to develop those resources and the legal framework that allows that capital to be able to come in place.

The second thing that Mexico is doing is it's proposed a very significant energy reform that would completely change the perspectives for private investment in conjunction or in joint ventures with PEMEX.

So if these things can begin to move forward and we see that there's a change in the legal environment with Mexico we have a North American hub that is contributor to energy supplies within our region. But frankly that's also a contributor to broader global energy security.

The reason I would underscore that as particularly important is that in the United States, particularly for oil, we pay global prices. We have a concern about what happens in global markets. If there isn't adequate supply to satisfy those international markets it has an impact on us in the United States of what we pay at the pump and for American economic productivity as well.

So for all of these reasons the kind of measure that's specifically addressed here in the Transboundary Agreement is reinforcing and supporting of that idea of American energy security. But it also is a foreshadowment of something which is even bigger of the potential for resurgence of North America as a whole to——

19

Senator MANCHIN. Let me ask this question.

Now basically with the area that we're talking about right now and I think they're estimating, Mr. Beaudreau, as that there's 172 million barrels of oil and 304 billion cubic feet of natural gas that you all have estimated. How did you come to that assessment?

Mr. BEAUDREAU. That assessment is based on analysis of the geology and the resource potential within that narrow transboundary strip. I honestly believe that the potential impacts of this agreement in terms of opening that area up and providing legal certainty will be broader than those statistics.

Senator MANCHIN. Let me ask this. Has Mexico been able to develop the deep drilling in the areas that they have control of?

Mr. BEAUDREAU. No.

Senator MANCHIN. I know we're talking about this area here mostly because for North America, for us the United States to be in there and work on agreements since it's kind of in no man's land, if you will. But has Mexico really developed to the potential they have?

Mr. BEAUDREAU. No. Ambassador Pascual should feel free to expand on it.

There is no production on the Mexican side of the transboundary, the maritime boundary. There is existing production in this geologic formation, the Perdido Fold Belt, in the Western Gulf on the U.S. side out of the Perdido hub. But the geology, as Ambassador Pascual described in his opening, is the same. There's lots of reason to think that it's highly perspective.

There have been 2 exploration wells drilled on the Mexican side by PEMEX. So they are in the area. They're interested in the area.

The question is whether we'll be there with them.

Senator MANCHIN. Let me just ask one more question, if I may?

The CHAIRMAN. Of course.

Senator MANCHIN. The average American at the pump has not seen relief every time that we do have this energy independence. We're finding more and more oil. We're finding shale gas. They have not seen the relief.

I know in my State of West Virginia we are not seeing the pump prices that are relative to what we're finding more energy in our country. I'm understanding that could be because of the refinery capacities that we have in our country.

Don't you think that maybe we could have a better relationship or kind of a joint relationship with Mexico, who probably is able to permit and build refineries that would help us have the supply we need in our country? Has that ever been explored to that extent, some kind of relationship there?

Mr. PASCUAL. Sir, the issue of how global markets and those global markets intersect back with our markets back in the United States are, as you say, a concern to Americans broadly and a concern to American productivity. So one of the realities is that the United States has supported generally free trade and free markets and as a result of that we pay international prices for oil.

So when the price of oil goes up to very high levels and it's been consistently at over $100 a barrel over the last 2 years and at times has gone to about $125 a barrel. It's now down to a little bit less than $110.

That has a direct impact.

Senator MANCHIN. Are there any options from pricing standpoint? If we're doing more and doing the heavy lift, if you will, more discovery, more technology, more of everything. We're not going to benefit because we're in this global pricing. Other countries haven't picked up the load or haven't done the heavy lifting or created new technologies.

Is there any chance for any relief for the United States of America and the people of this country to have the benefits of this?

Mr. PASCUAL. The critical thing to benefit the American people has been to get sufficient and adequate supplies on global markets to be able to balance those markets. The alternative would be to have to subsidize energy prices.

The United States has not supported that. It has not supported the subsidies for fossil fuels. So it obviously would be another impact on the budget to be able to do that.

So the approach that has been taken is to encourage as much private investment as possible, the conditions for private investment, so companies from the United States, from around the world, can develop those energy resources.

Fortunately the American companies have been in a leadership role and being able to do that. It's created significant jobs as a result of that for those companies for the American service industries.

Senator MANCHIN. But little relief.

Mr. PASCUAL. Then brought that back to the United States.

Senator MANCHIN. But very little relief, wouldn't you agree?

Mr. PASCUAL. Pardon me?

Senator MANCHIN. Very little relief.

Mr. PASCUAL. In terms of broader impact on energy prices.

Senator MANCHIN. To the consumer.

Mr. PASCUAL. It has not changed those.

Senator MANCHIN. So someone is doing extremely well.

Mr. PASCUAL. Pardon me?

Senator MANCHIN. Someone is doing financially extremely well?

Mr. PASCUAL. There are certainly many companies that have benefited financially from——

Senator MANCHIN. I don't—I'm not faulting that.

I'm just saying sooner or later the consumer has got to win one. Just one. Right now they're not.

You're going to open this up and open that up and all these things are going to be great and helpful. But if it's not going to give this relief how do you go home and sell it to the people to get support?

That's the problem we have, sir.

I'm so sorry. I went over my time, sir. I'm sorry.

The CHAIRMAN. I thank my colleague. This discussion of how the relief is actually going to make its way to people at the pump is something that is going to be continued and focused on very aggressively by this committee in the months ahead because certainly as people talk about production and then people pull up to the neighborhood station and still feel like they're getting mugged trying to afford to fill their tank is an increasingly important question.

Now, here's where we are.

I'm going to do everything I can to pass this agreement quickly and cleanly. I think you all have done a very good job. I appreciate the answer that you gave to Senator Landrieu's question so that the agreement will in fact apply to the important statute she authored, the GOMESA Act.

We'll probably be talking to you about additional questions. But we're going to do everything we can to move this quickly and cleanly. We appreciate your good work and we'll excuse you at this time.

Mr. BEAUDREAU. Thank you.

The CHAIRMAN. Let's now bring forward Ms. Jacqueline Savitz, Vice President, U.S. Oceans, Oceana.

Mr. Erik Milito, Director, Upstream and Industry Operations, the American Petroleum Institute.

Alright. We welcome both of you.

We have Ms. Jacqueline Savitz, Vice President, U.S. Oceans, Oceana. We've worked with you all often.

Ms. SAVITZ. Yes, sir.

The CHAIRMAN. Not in the years past. Appreciate the good work you're doing.

Mr. Erik Milito, Director Upstream and Industry Operations, American Petroleum Institute. Often ask for your views on issues.

So we'll make your prepared remarks a part of the record in their entirety. I know there's always a compulsion to almost just read every word. If you can just summarize your views that would be great.

Let's begin with you, Ms. Savitz.

STATEMENT OF JACQUELINE SAVITZ, VICE PRESIDENT, U.S. OCEANS, OCEANA

Ms. SAVITZ. Thank you, Chairman Wyden, good morning. Morning, Ranking Member Murkowski. Thank you for the opportunity to testify here today.

My name is Jacqueline Savitz and I'm the Vice President for U.S. Oceans for Oceana. We're a global ocean conservation organization and we're dedicated to restoring and protecting the world's oceans.

Oceana believes that offshore drilling should not be expanded. For that reason we oppose S. 812 and H.R. 1613. There are 3 primary reasons which I'll summarize for you today.

First, the presumption that more oil and gas is better should not drive our energy policy. Instead we should embrace and promote the needed shift away from fossil fuels and toward clean energy which will benefit Americans today and also future generations. This means making more strategic investments to move away from dirty and dangerous fuels that present major risks both in terms of their current production practices and their long term impacts on climate.

The science shows clearly that fossil fuels like oil and gas are driving climate change which threatens to bring us famine, drought, increased storm frequency and intensity, sea level rise and ocean acidification. Thus scientific bodies like the International Energy Agency have recommended that much of our oil reserves ultimately must be left in the ground to avert the worst impacts of climate change.

Our second concern is that the agreement fails to satisfy a basic cost benefit analysis as it brings a tremendous amount of risk of devastating spills and climate impacting results with little benefit. The agreement does not adequately address the safety risks associated with oil and gas development and current Federal requirements do not provide an effective backstop. Both bills are silent on environmental protections and the agreements suggest protections where appropriate or where necessary which is a recipe for disaster.

A spill from one rig, like the Deepwater Horizon, would be devastating to fisheries and tourism economies both in the U.S. and in Mexico, not to mention the ecosystem itself. The revenues don't come close to making up for it.

The oil that we will produce as a result of this agreement would supply us for about 4 and a half days. The natural gas would supply only about 2 days of our natural gas demands. In exchange we risk another major oil spill like Ixtoc or the more recent Deepwater Horizon disaster.

Since that accident Congress has not passed a single new safety requirement. The new rules that have come out of the Department of the Interior are not sufficient.

They fail to require sufficient technology.

They rely on technology with design flaws like blow out preventers which third parties have found to have design flaws.

They're undercut by minimal penalties and willfully inadequate inspections and enforcement.

Liability limits also remain inadequate with no fix in sight.

So the risk that would result from production in transboundary area are not justified by the benefits.

Our third concern is that the continued emphasis on expanded offshore drilling is slowing the necessary investment in clean energy, clean energy development, which would stimulate the economy, I'm sorry, which would stimulate the economy without the intended risks and would also help to alleviate the worst impacts of climate change. Alternative energy sources like solar and offshore wind promise to mitigate climate change impacts while providing jobs and stimulating the economy as much, if not more, than fossil fuels would.

According to the Department of Energy the U.S. has more than 4,000 gigawatts of offshore wind energy potential. This is enough energy to power the U.S. 4 times over. This abundant domestic resource could support up to 200,000 manufacturing, construction and operation jobs across the country and drive over 70 billion in annual investments by 2030.

Developing even 10 percent of this clean energy resource for just 1 year, 10 percent, would produce at least 25 times more energy than developing all of the oil and gas in the transboundary area and unlike that oil the wind will continue to produce clean energy year after year.

The choice is clear for our children and our grandchildren. We need to shift away from fossil fuels and toward clean energy. This bill takes us in the wrong direction.

Expanding drilling to areas that are hard to reach or difficult to negotiate like the U.S./Mexico Transboundary areas will leave us with a continued dependence on dirty and dangerous energy sources and severe climate impacts in exchange for very little actual energy. There's a better energy strategy and Congress should lead us in a new direction.

Thank you.

[The prepared statement of Ms. Savitz follows:]

PREPARED STATEMENT OF JACQUELINE SAVITZ, VICE PRESIDENT, US. OCEANS, OCEANA

Introduction

Good morning Mr. Chairman and members of the committee. Thank you for the opportunity to testify today. My name is Jacqueline Savitz, and I am Vice President for U.S. Oceans for Oceana, a global ocean conservation organization based here in Washington, D.C., that works to restore and protect the world's oceans. Besides our headquarters in Washington D.C., Oceana has international operations in Belgium, Denmark, Spain, Belize and Chile. Here in the U.S. beyond our D.C. operations, we have staff located in Alaska, Oregon, California, Maine, New York, Virginia, South Carolina and Florida. We have 750,000 members and supporters from all 50 states and from countries around the globe. Our mission is to protect our oceans and the fish and wildlife that depend on them.

Oceana opposes S.812, and its counterpart in the House, H.R.1613, for three reasons.

First, we do not believe that drilling operations should be expanded. Expanding offshore drilling is unnecessary and dangerous, especially when we haven't yet fully addressed the risks. Besides the obvious impacts of oil exploration, production, refining, and transportation, the use of oil and gas is also problematic as these fossil fuels are contributing to climate change. Our continued expansion of their use is unnecessary and wrong-headed. In order to combat global climate change, we should be transitioning off of fossil fuels in favor of clean, renewable energy development.

Second, our continued emphasis on expanding offshore drilling is slowing the necessary investment in clean energy projects that will stimulate the economy without the attendant risks, and help to alleviate the worst impacts of climate change.

Lastly, the "Agreement between the United States and Mexico Concerning Transboundary Hydrocarbon Reservoirs in Gulf of Mexico" ("Agreement") fails to satisfy a basic cost-benefit analysis, as it brings a tremendous amount of risk of devastating spills, and climate impacting results, with little concomitant benefit. The Agreement itself does not adequately address the safety risks associated with oil and gas development, and current federal requirements do not provide an effective backstop. The agreement also fails to provide significant benefits to the United States, beyond what we can be getting from clean energy. The risks of the expanded drilling called for in the Agreement far outweigh the rewards. Rather than opening this area to new and expanded oil and gas production, we believe that the moratorium on drilling in the transboundary area should be continued, and that the U.S. should invest further in stimulating the development of offshore wind and other clean energy opportunities.

WE SHOULD NOT EXPAND OFFSHORE DRILLING

The proposed expansion of offshore drilling is unnecessary and dangerous, and we haven't yet fully addressed the risks. The federal government's most recent Five-Year Plan allows access to more than 75 percent of estimated undiscovered technically recoverable oil and gas resources on the U.S. Outer Continental Shelf. At the same time, the oil and gas industry is sitting on a large number of non-producing leases in federal waters. According to a July 2013 U.S. Department of the Interior report, oil and gas companies hold almost 6,000 active leases in the Gulf, 82 percent of which are non-producing leases. This represents more than ample opportunity for exploration and development and certainly more than we would get by expanding drilling to the transboundary area. Additionally, even if all of the oil available in the transboundary area were to be extracted and the U.S. recovered the entirety of the reserve, this amount would be less than one-half percent of the total amount of technically recoverable oil currently available in the Gulf of Mexico (specifically, 0.37 percent). Couple this with the fact that our continued reliance on fossil fuels is exacerbating global climate change and it is hard to find the logic in expanding offshore drilling to the transboundary area when there is so little benefit for us in return.

DRILLING IS NOT SAFE

Following the Deepwater Horizon disaster, the newly created Bureau of Offshore Energy Management, Regulation and Enforcement ("BOEMRE") issued three sets of new safety regulations in an effort to increase offshore drilling safety and to prevent a similar disaster from happening again. Following the initial release of the new safety regulations, Oceana conducted an exhaustive review which looked at every new requirement to assess the degree to which they would improve safety. We found that these new rules simply did not take necessary steps to minimize risks, and further, would not prevent us from having another catastrophic spill.

The new rules suffer from their own shortcomings, and any positive benefit new safety regulations might offer are undermined by systemic problems that have yet to be corrected. These include an inadequate inspection capacity and an insufficient penalty structure which leads to continued economic incentives to cut corners and ignore requirements.

SAFETY MEASURES PUT IN PLACE SINCE DEEPWATER HORIZON FAIL TO MAKE DRILLING SAFE

The Final Drilling Safety Rule

The provisions of the Final Drilling Safety Rule can be divided into three categories: training and maintenance, equipment testing, and well design and equipment. While many of these regulations represent positive reforms that are an improvement over the regulations in place during Deepwater Horizon, the Final Drilling Safety Rule's effort to increase safety is undermined by systemic problems in offshore regulation and by serious shortcomings in the rule itself.

Training Maintenance

Improved maintenance and training are both positive reforms that can reduce chances of equipment failure and operator error and thus increase safety. Yet of all the provisions in the Final Drilling Safety Rule, training and maintenance regulations are the most dependent on the robustness of BSEE's oversight and inspection capabilities. Maintenance is an ongoing concern that necessitates being frequently checked and inspected and training is only valuable if it translates into appropriate actions, which also requires continuous oversight to ensure safety regulations are properly met. Unfortunately, BSEE's oversight and inspection programs are woefully inadequate and civil penalties are far too small to ensure compliance and deter risk-taking by the industry. These systemic problems undermine the Final Drilling Safety Rule's efforts to increase offshore safety through new training and maintenance requirements. Ensuring the efficacy of many of the new rules would require a much stronger inspection and oversight program than what currently exists.

Equipment Testing

BSEE has implemented numerous new equipment testing requirements that apply to various stages in offshore drilling. These testing requirements might seem to improve the safety of offshore drilling; however, they are also undermined by BSEE's inadequate inspection program and by insufficient civil penalties that create a perverse economic incentive to skip or ignore tests to save time.

Well Design and Equipment

The Final Drilling Safety Rule requires drilling wells to be equipped with two independent barriers to flow. If correctly installed, these barriers could in fact protect against blowouts. However, the requirements for two barriers to flow can easily be undermined by operator error. This problem is illustrated by the Deepwater Horizon disaster, where a cement job, a common barrier to flow, was compromised by numerous operator errors. With limited funds for inspection and oversight, and perverse economics that incentivize project speed over safety, it is likely that not all barriers will be properly installed.

No New Blowout Preventer Rule

BSEE still has yet to implement its new safety rule on blowout preventer technology. Blowout preventers are used to seal a well in the case of a blowout or a loss of well control. They provide the last line of defense against offshore drilling blowouts. Both the National Commission on the BP Deepwater Horizon Oil Spill and Offshore Drilling and the National Academy of Engineering have recommended that blowout preventers be redesigned in light of flaws uncovered by the Deepwater Horizon oil spill. Unfortunately, this has not been done. While some new testing and maintenance regulations for blowout preventers have been enacted, these neither address nor fix the underlying design flaws. Furthermore, simple requirements that would improve the odds that a blowout preventer functions correctly and seals the well—such as requiring redundancy in its shearing rams or testing blowout preventers under real-life conditions—have not been required. As a result of the government's inaction in this area, blowout preventers being used throughout the Gulf of Mexico and elsewhere are at risk of failing just as the Deepwater Horizon's did. Failure by the government and the industry to ensure the effectiveness of blowout prevention technology is problematic, but continuing to allow and even expand drilling, especially in deep water, in spite of this failure is absolutely unacceptable.

Oversight and Inspection Levels are Paltry Relative to the Scale of Drilling Operations

Since the Deepwater Horizon disaster there has not been a sufficient increase in the number of federal inspectors or the size of penalties. While the Bureau of Safety and Environmental Enforcement ("BSEE") has attempted to strengthen its inspection and oversight capabilities, funding levels remain far below what would be needed for frequent and thorough inspections that would reduce instances of equipment failure and operator error. Low inspection rates not only undermine regulatory compliance by reducing the odds that violations will be observed, but also limit real-time monitoring of operations by inspectors, a necessary prerequisite to avert disasters as problems are difficult to foresee even a few days before they occur. This creates a perverse incentive for operators to risk violations when doing so can save them time and/or money, rather than properly following the new safety regulations, because they are unlikely to be caught.

The United States is far behind the rest of the developed world when it comes to inspectors available and trained to inspect the oil and gas rigs off our coasts. The number of inspectors per offshore oil rig in other developed countries is as follows: in the U.K., the inspector to rig ratio is 1: 2.78; in Norway, the inspector to rig ratio is 1:1.05; in the U.S., the inspector to rig ratio is 1:29. We are playing Russian roulette with our offshore drilling operations by not having a sufficient inspection program and thus, even BSEE's new safety requirements cannot make offshore drilling significantly safer or decrease the chances of an oil spill.

Violating Rules Can be Lucrative Because Penalties Remain Small

BSEE's civil penalties are too small to ensure compliance and deter risk taken by the oil and gas industry. The maximum penalty BOEM can assess for civil violations is $40,000 per day per violation. In comparison, BP was paying over $500,000 per day to use the Deepwater Horizon rig, and total estimated daily operating costs of the operation were approximately $1 million. This disparity between penalties for violating regulations and operating costs creates a perverse incentive for drillers to cut corners and complete operations in a timely rather than safe manner. Indeed, Former Director of BOEMRE Michael Bromwich expressed a similar sentiment in testimony delivered to the House Natural Resources Committee, stating that "the current enforcement framework, which permits maximum fines of only $40,000 per day, per incident, is patently inadequate to deter violations in an environment where drilling operations can cost more than a million dollars a day."

The driller can risk a violation in part because they are unlikely to be caught and penalized, in part due to BSEE's inadequate inspection capabilities, and also because even if they are caught, the penalty is so low that it may pay to break the rules. Raising the maximum fine BSEE can assess for civil penalties to a level comparable with operational costs would eliminate the perverse financial incentive for corner-cutting and increase the likelihood offshore operators comply with the new safety regulations. Raising the penalty would have to be done by Congress, as BSEE is legally constrained in how many times and to what extent it can raise penalty sizes. As long as rule-breaking pays, new rules cannot protect us from a spill.

At the time of the disaster, the Administration stated that it would not allow drilling to resume unless safety concerns were addressed. Yet drilling was allowed to resume in spite of the lack of sufficient safety regulations. We believe this was a mistake in itself. However, further expansion of oil and gas development, as is envisioned by H.R.1613 and S.812, is clearly wrong-headed, and is a set up for another drilling disaster like the Deepwater Horizon or IXTOC events.

CLIMATE CONSIDERATIONS

In May, for the first time in history, the Earth's atmospheric carbon dioxide levels reached 400 parts per million (ppm). This ominous milestone is a stark reminder of what our continued dependence on fossil fuels is doing to our planet. Such dangerous levels of carbon dioxide in the atmosphere are bringing us ever closer to the point of no return and we are already witnessing its disastrous effects. Hurricanes, tornados, tropical storms, and "superstorms" have increased in both severity and frequency. Not only have these storms resulted in the loss of human life and irrevocable property damage, but they have also gotten increasingly expensive, costing billions of dollars in taxpayer money to clean up devastated towns and cities in the U.S. and elsewhere.

These storms are the alarm bells of climate change. We need to act swiftly and immediately to drastically reduce the level of carbon dioxide we are pumping into the Earth's atmosphere. A 2012 report from the International Energy Agency (IEA) held that extreme consequences of climate change would be associated with a 2 degree Celsius warming. As the world's authority on global energy trends, the IEA concluded that in order to achieve a goal of keeping warming under 2 degrees Celsius, two-thirds of our fossil fuel reserves—oil, natural gas and coal—need to stay in the ground as opposed to being released into our atmosphere through production and use as fuel. Instead of doubling down on drilling which will push us past these climatic tipping points, we should heed the warnings of these experts and begin the swift transition from fossil fuels to clean, renewable energy.

Offshore wind can be a big part of this transition, as the scale of America's offshore wind energy resource is truly staggering, with literally thousands of gigawatts (GW) of clean energy available off our shores. For over 20 years, Europe has been generating clean energy and jobs from its offshore wind resource. In fact, there are 1,700 offshore turbines spinning at 55 offshore wind farms overseas, generating approximately 5 GW of electricity. Yet, the U.S. remains stalled with no wind farms in the water at all to date.

According to the DOE's 2011 report, "A National Offshore Wind Strategy: Creating an Offshore Wind Energy Industry in the United States," the U.S. has over 4,000 GW of gross offshore wind energy potential off its coasts. As former Secretary of the Interior Ken Salazar has repeatedly noted, that is enough energy to power the U.S. four times over.

Also according to the DOE, a U.S. offshore wind industry that takes advantage of this abundant domestic resource could support up to 200,000 manufacturing, construction, operation and supply chain jobs across the country and drive over $70 billion in annual investments by 2030. Offshore wind represents an economic and energy opportunity that could mirror, and even surpass, the success of land-based wind development. If the U.S. develops even 10 percent of this clean energy resource for one year, we would produce about 25 times more energy than we would if we developed all of the oil and gas in the transboundary area, and unlike oil, offshore wind will continue to produce clean energy year after year after year.

WE MUST MAKE A SWIFT TRANSITION FROM FOSSIL FUELS TO CLEAN ENERGY

Our continued emphasis on expanding drilling is preventing us from the needed investment in clean energy that would stimulate the economy without the risks associated with drilling and would also help to alleviate the worst impacts of climate change. As I said earlier, in order to combat global climate change, we need to focus on transitioning off of fossil fuels in favor of clean, renewable energy development. Offshore wind can be a big part of this transition, though as with all burgeoning industries, one of the biggest impediments to this clean energy development is financing. In order for a domestic offshore wind industry to get up and running, a long-term extension of the Investment Tax Credit (ITC) is needed. To that end, Senators Tom Carper and Susan Collins have introduced S.401, the Incentivizing Offshore Wind Power Act, bipartisan legislation that will extend the ITC to the first 3,000 MW of offshore wind installed. This extension will provide much-needed certainty to investors, which will make offshore wind an affordable, viable investment and will ultimately help to catapult this burgeoning industry into the mainstream. This is the type of legislation that can help solve our energy and environmental challenges, without risking lives and livelihoods, as well as marine ecosystems. A focus on promoting clean energy could get us all the benefits of the Agreement and more, without the risks.

THE AGREEMENT FAILS TO ADDRESS ENVIRONMENTAL CONCERNS

The Agreement fails to adequately address the safety risks of drilling and is effectively silent on environmental protection. As such, this agreement provides little to no additional benefit to the U.S., especially compared to what we could be getting from clean energy. In a recent Congressional Research Service (CRS) report done on this topic, entitled, "Proposed U.S.-Mexico Transboundary Hydrocarbons Agreement: Background and Issues for Congress," BOEM estimates that there are 172 million barrels of oil and 304 billion cubic feet of natural gas in the transboundary area. As this is the total amount of oil and gas in the transboundary area, the U.S. would only be entitled to half. According to the EIA, the U.S. consumed 18.83 million barrels of oil per day in 2011 and consumed 25.46 trillion cubic feet of natural gas per day in 2012. Therefore, at maximum extraction and assuming the U.S. and

Mexico split these reserves evenly, the oil that the U.S. would get as a result of this agreement would supply only about 4 ° days of our total oil demands and the natural gas that the U.S. would get would supply only about 2 days of our natural gas demands. Additionally, the same CRS report states that the U.S. would only bring in $50 million from energy activities projected to take place in the transboundary area, as compared to $6.9 billion in revenue the U.S. got from offshore energy production in 2012 alone. To put this in perspective, this paltry sum would represent less than 1 percent (0.72 percent, to be exact) of the total offshore revenues of the U.S.

Lastly, there seems to be little to no thought put into what kind of environmental protections would be required in the transboundary area. For instance, both H.R.1613 and S.812 are silent on environmental protections for the area and the Agreement merely suggests protections "where appropriate" or "where necessary," which provides absolutely no mandate and is totally open to interpretation. Expanding the risky and dangerous practice of offshore drilling to an area where no thought or consideration is given to environmental protections is a recipe for disaster. It is unacceptable to move forward with such an endeavor when even the safety regulations we currently have in place would not adequately prevent another Deepwater Horizon oil spill disaster.

CONCLUSION

Oceana opposes implementation of the Agreement because: (1) we do not believe that drilling operations should be expanded; (2) the continued emphasis on expanded offshore drilling is slowing the necessary investment in clean energy projects that would stimulate the economy and help to alleviate the worst impacts of climate change; and (3) the Agreement fails to satisfy a basic risk/benefit analysis, as it brings a tremendous amount of risk of devastating spills and climate impacting results, with relatively little concomitant benefit.

The risks of the expanded drilling called for in the Agreement far outweigh the rewards. Rather than opening this area to new and expanded oil and gas production, we believe that the moratorium on drilling in the transboundary area should be extended, and that the U.S. should invest further in stimulating the development of offshore wind and other clean energy opportunities.

Thank you for your time. I'm happy to answer any questions you may have.

The CHAIRMAN. Very good. Thank you.
Mr. Milito.

STATEMENT OF ERIK MILITO, GROUP DIRECTOR, UPSTREAM AND INDUSTRY OPERATIONS, AMERICAN PETROLEUM INSTITUTE

Mr. MILITO. Good morning, Chairman Wyden, Senator Murkowski. I'm Erik Milito, Upstream Director of the American Petroleum Institute. Thank you for the opportunity to appear today for you as a witness.

API has more than 500 member companies which represent all sectors of America's oil and natural industry. Our industry supports 9.8 million American jobs and 8 percent of the U.S. economy.

The industry also provides most of the energy we need to power our economy and way of life and delivers more than $85 million a day in revenue to the Federal Government.

Our Nation can and should be producing more of the oil and natural gas Americans need here at home. This would strengthen our energy security and help put downward pressure on prices while also providing many thousands of new jobs for Americans and billions of dollars in additional revenue for our government.

According to Energy Information Administration statistics we produced a little more than 5 million barrels of oil a day in 2009 and are projected to produce nearly 9 million barrels a day by the end of 2014. We are simultaneously reducing the amount of oil that we import. But we can and should do more.

The Gulf of Mexico oil and gas development supports approximately 400 thousand jobs throughout the U.S. economy with one-fourth of those jobs in States outside the Gulf region. I'd like to point out that a recent study that Quest Offshore Drilling conducted shows that these jobs that support the Gulf reach all through the country. There are companies. There are vendors in Oregon and places as far as Alaska when it comes to supporting Gulf production. So it's significant that it's not just Gulf States that benefit.

The Transboundary Hydrocarbon Agreement with Mexico is important as it could help create additional revenue opportunities for U.S. oil and natural gas companies in the Gulf of Mexico. In turn create more jobs and enhance our energy security. The Agreement establishes a cooperative process for managing oil and gas reservoirs along the boundary region in the Gulf of Mexico and encourages cooperative agreements with U.S. independent oil companies and Mexico's State owned oil company to jointly develop energy resources along the boundary areas.

Importantly this agreement will provide legal certainty to U.S. companies which will encourage them to invest in new energy development creating jobs and spurring economic growth.

Implementing legislation authorizing this important agreement should be approved as quickly as possible. S. 812 takes that pivotal step. Swift implementation of the Transboundary Hydrocarbon Agreement is important to providing regulatory certainty and will allow companies to make investments in these boundary areas with the knowledge that there is a framework in place to allow for orderly extraction of these resources.

Given that industry investments in the offshore are largely limited to the Gulf of Mexico, this will serve to enhance our Nation's energy security and long term economic growth and highlight the importance of national leadership in promoting a positive forward looking energy policy.

The last thing I'd like to add is that the oil and natural gas industry is comprised of energy companies, that our focus is on oil and natural gas. That's what they're good at. That's what they've been doing for this country for a long time.

From 2012—from 2007 to 2012 according to EIA the extraction side, the exploration and production side actually increased jobs by 40 percent. So it's a significant driver of employment here in this country.

But I would add to that that they are energy companies. A recent study by T2 and Associates found that from 2000 to 2012 the oil and gas industry invested approximately $81 billion into GHG mitigating technologies. Whereas other industries combined invested an estimated $91 million—$91 billion and the Federal Government invested an estimated $79 billion.

In that same timeframe the oil and natural gas industry was responsible for approximately 17 percent or $11.4 billion of all investments in non hydrocarbon resources including wind, solar, geothermal and biomass technologies. So these are energy companies. These are companies that have done a great job of finding oil and gas resources so that we have them here in the United States and we can drive economic recovery and economic growth but at the same time I don't think you can ignore the fact that the energy companies have been doing their fair share to try to drive investment in non hydrocarbon resources. Just want to put that out there.

Appreciate the opportunity once again to appear before you and be able to provide my testimony. I'm happy to answer any questions.

[The prepared statement of Mr. Milito follows:]

PREPARED STATEMENT OF ERIK MILITO, GROUP DIRECTOR, UPSTREAM AND INDUSTRY OPERATIONS, AMERICAN PETROLEUM INSTITUTE

Good morning Chairman Wyden, Senator Murkowski, and members of the committee. I am Erik Milito, Upstream Director at the American Petroleum Institute.

API has more than 500 member companies, which represent all sectors of America's oil and natural gas industry. Our industry supports 9.8 million American jobs and 8.0 percent of the U.S. economy. The industry also provides most of the energy we need to power our economy and way of life and delivers more than $85 million a day in revenue to the federal government.

Our nation can and should be producing more of the oil and natural gas Americans need here at home. This would strengthen our energy security and help put downward pressure on prices while also providing many thousands of new jobs for Americans and billions of dollars in additional revenue for our government. According to Energy Information Administration statistics, we produced a little more than 5 million barrels of oil a day in 2009 and are projected to produce nearly 9 million barrels a day by the end of 2014. We are simultaneously reducing the amount of oil that we import. But we can and should do more.

Gulf of Mexico oil and gas development supports approximately 400,000 jobs throughout the U.S. economy, with one-fourth of those jobs in states outside the Gulf region. The Transboundary Hydrocarbon Agreement with Mexico is important as it could help create additional resource opportunities for U.S. oil and natural gas companies in the Gulf of Mexico and in turn create more jobs and enhance our energy security. The agreement establishes a cooperative process for managing oil and gas reservoirs along the boundary region in the Gulf of Mexico and encourages cooperative agreements between U.S. independent oil companies (IOCs) and Mexico's state-owned oil company (Pemex) to jointly develop energy resources along boundary areas in the Gulf of Mexico. Importantly, this agreement will provide legal certainty to U.S. companies, which will encourage them to invest in new energy development, creating jobs and spurring economic growth.

The importance of this agreement is magnified by the fact that the administration has chosen a status quo approach to offshore oil and natural gas development that restricts oil and gas development to portions of the Gulf of Mexico and Alaska and leaves approximately 87 percent of Outer Continental Shelf areas off limits. We continue to hear about an "all-of-the above" energy approach and the administration's projections show that oil and natural gas will supply most of the nation's energy for decades to come. However, we need to see real action in order to ensure that we are effectively meeting the nation's need for continued oil and gas resources to fuel our economy. Approval of the U.S.—Mexico Transboundary Agreement is one way that we can create and encourage additional opportunities for safe and environmentally responsible domestic energy production on federal land.

Implementing legislation authorizing this important agreement should be approved as quickly as possible, and S. 812 takes that pivotal step. Swift implementation of the Transboundary Hydrocarbon Agreement is important to providing regulatory certainty and will allow companies to make investments in these boundary areas with the knowledge that there is a framework in place to allow for orderly extraction of these resources. Given that industry investments in the offshore are largely limited to the Gulf of Mexico, this will serve to enhance our nation's energy security and long-term economic growth and highlight the importance of national leadership in promoting a positive, forward-looking energy policy.

Thank you again to the Chairman and the Committee and I look forward to your questions.

The CHAIRMAN. Thank you both. Very helpful.

Let me begin with you, if I could, Ms. Savitz. As you know we've worked with your organization many times. I have enormous respect for Mr. Danzig, who we worked with you on over fishing.

Certainly when you talk about climate change you've got me at hello. I mean this 400 parts per million finding recently—that ought to be a wakeup call to everybody.

So we're going to be focused very specifically on ways to promote a lower carbon economy. There are a whole host of ways to do it.

The question that I really have is how is having no agreement better than having an agreement/ Let me kind of be specific about this.

My understanding is without an agreement Mexico can proceed on their own. Should they do it and they're talking about changing their Constitution and the like. You could have, you know, ultra deep drilling and you could have a whole host of areas that wouldn't be subject to the kind of government standards we're talking about here in terms of safety and environmental protection, so fewer platforms, that sort of thing.

Tell me your view about why no agreement is in effect better than this agreement.

Ms. SAVITZ. Thank you, sir. Let me start by saying thank you back to you. Likewise we've enjoyed very much working with you and with the Ranking Member on a variety of different issues. We'll continue to do so.

Thank you for your sentiments on climate change. It's a huge problem for the oceans. It's leading to ocean acidification. Scientists are predicting that by mid century we'll start to see mass extinctions of coral reefs around the world. Mid century, really, unfortunately, is not that far away which is why we've been pushing so hard to try to get a shift in the way we think about energy and shifting away from fossil fuels and toward clean energy which provides us a solution to those problems.

From our perspective the best case scenario in the U.S./Mexico Agreement would be for the United States to lead Mexico in that direction rather than facilitating or enabling the development of this area by both the United States and Mexico. I think there's some questions about what, you know, what Mexico will do in the absence of the agreement. But it's also not clear that Mexico will develop this area and that we couldn't be facilitating that development without necessarily opening up additional areas to offshore drilling.

The CHAIRMAN. Alright.

One question for you, if I might, Mr. Milito.

Part of the reason there's been a moratorium in the Western Gap has been due to concern of drainage of resources from one side of the transboundary from the other. This concern, of course, is dealt with in the agreement by the implementation of unitization agreements. Senator Murkowski has already referred to them.

These are agreements among lessees to develop a common reservoir and allocate production jointly. Are you satisfied that this provision deals adequately with this issue? Again, what are the consequences if there's no agreement?

Mr. MILITO. Yes, we are. In the way it works out currently for even U.S. producers in the Gulf of Mexico is that if you have a reservoir that crosses leases companies have to enter and normally do enter into unitization agreements so that there is an agreement in place to ensure that production is being allocated and that the reservoir is being managed according to an underlying agreement.

So that history in practice is there. Then when going forward to develop the cross boundary reservoirs that overlap between the U.S. and Mexico boundary, we now have the certainty in place to allow companies to do a similar, enter into similar agreements, when it comes to dealing with PEMEX and making sure that there is the certainty in place from a legal standpoint to move forward and have that production allocated and have those royalties and revenues divided up as outlined in the underlying unitization agreements.

So that certainty is provided through this Transboundary Agreement.

The CHAIRMAN. Very good.

Senator Murkowski.

Senator MURKOWSKI. Thank you, Mr. Chairman.

To both of you, thank you for your testimony here this morning. Appreciate it.

Ms. Savitz, you, in answer to the chairman's question, you've indicated that the concern is a bigger picture just trying to move away from fossil fuel. I think he tried to indicate that if this agreement does move forward what we do is we set in place a framework for joint development, making sure that that footprint is smaller, promoting common safety, environmental standards.

Is there anything that you can think of that would, I guess, enhance the terms of the agreement so that Oceana would actually support this agreement or are you opposed under all circumstances? I guess I'm trying to understand if there are areas that could be enhanced that would cause you to revisit this?

Ms. SAVITZ. Thank you for that question. I think it's a very thoughtful question.

One of the big concerns we have with the agreement is it's very unclear to us from the agreement where the, you know, what safety standards would be required for offshore drilling of Mexico. We kind of know what safety standards are required in the United States. It's not clear to us that our safety standards necessarily would be recognized and respected or that we would have any authority to guarantee them.

But in addition to that we're also very concerned with the status of the existing safety requirements for offshore drilling.

We don't think they're sufficient.

They don't require sufficient technology.

There's a serious lack of funding for inspections.

They're very low penalties that even former head of BOEMRE, Michael Bromwich, you know, was very concerned about the low penalties. So essentially what we get is even though we have some standards they're not necessarily being met and that the standards aren't strong enough.

We have a liability cap in place. It hasn't been lifted since Deepwater Horizon. So there's a variety of things that a, we're not sure that the Mexican drilling company would recognize our standards.

Even if they did we're not satisfied with the strength of our standards.

Senator MURKOWSKI. Let me ask you, Mr. Milito, whether or not your members, the folks that are affiliated or associated with API are currently working with Mexico on oil and gas safety technology, environmental issues. Do you have a level of collaboration that is ongoing related to oil and gas development in the Gulf right now?

Mr. MILITO. Thank you, Senator. That's an interesting question considering that just a few weeks ago we had hosted a delegation of Senators from Mexico who came to API to learn about what we're doing here in the United States. So we took that opportunity in conjunction with that State Department, being able to line that meeting up to kind of go through what we were doing as an industry here in the United States and outlining a lot of the work we've done in terms of raising and enhancing the level of performance in offshore operations in terms of preventing an accident, containing one and responding to one.

It appeared very clear from that discussion that there is a strong desire from the Mexican government to be able to move forward and get its production increased back up. But it's important to make sure that we're doing it in a safe and environmentally responsible way.

Our industry also has been working closely with BSEE and BOEM and then also speaking before forums like the International Regulators Forum to make sure that we are disseminating and spreading the information about robust regulatory frameworks and high level standards that should be employed throughout the world. Our companies on a one on one basis also work with Mexico and Mexican authorities to make sure that all this information and the technologies and standards are being communicated across borders.

So I think we're doing what we can. I think a lot of that is also being handled through both the BOEM, BSEE and the State Department.

Thank you.

Senator MURKOWSKI. You know, you can't help but think about or I can't help but think coming from Alaska that when we talk about development in our oceans it—the issues are different. When you're on land and you know where your State boundaries are it's just a little bit different dynamic. What we're trying to do up North in a very evolving part of the world, is a recognition that in the Arctic Nations there is greater efforts of collaboration whether it is with environmental issues, whether it's in search and rescue, whether it is oil spill prevention and just the whole preparedness.

But it's one thing when it's the U.S. talking to our neighbors just to the south in Mexico. It's another thing when you've got multiple countries that you are dealing with where standards might be a little bit different.

So appreciate your response to that.

Can you speak and this is to you, Mr. Milito again, to the level of interest within the membership of API in developing these oil and gas resources that are along the transboundary area? Mr. Beaudreau mentioned that there have been applicants or perspective lease holders that have stepped forward but his suggestion was that once this uncertainty is resolved or excuse me, once this moratorium is resolved that there will be a greater interest in activity in that area.

Can you speak to that?

Mr. MILITO. Yes. That's our understanding as well is that given the inability to move forward with legal certainty that companies No. 1, have not been able to move forward and apply for permits and actually go out there and engage in initial exploratory activities. But, you know, they haven't been able to also put forward a strong forward looking program to tap into these opportunities from a broader standpoint.

I do think that when you look at the map which shows you where the lease blocks are, you will see a production platform like Perdido which has capacity for 100 thousand barrels a day. Not far from this area and you see selectively companies who have bid on and purchases leases right along that border that there is interest there. Not given that we're a trade association and this is a lot of confidential business information. We're not privy to a lot of that information.

But it's clear that the industry as a whole would like to look at these perspective areas and determine what's there and whether there are opportunities to then move into the production stage. So it's step by step by step, but given that the Gulf of Mexico is a very mature area it's areas like this that would allow this Nation to enhance its own energy security.

Senator MURKOWSKI. Appreciate it. Thank you, Mr. Chairman.

The CHAIRMAN. Thank you, Senator Murkowski.

You know, what I'm struck by particularly as we wrap up, and I know we were very pleased to get the helium legislation passed last week because there would have been real consequences, essentially starting this week, in terms of millions of jobs being affected, 700,000 MRIs each week that need that liquid helium to be able to cool those super conducting magnets. Back when everybody started talking about helium I think I mentioned to you I thought that helium was about balloons.

We really under—we've learned a lot. Thank you for your cooperation. I think we've got to bring the same kind of urgency to this agreement as well.

What I'm struck by is January 17th, basically means that the moratorium expires. It's kind of first come, first serve. It's open season.

As I was really touching on with you, Ms. Savitz, and this is recognizing all the good work that you all do at your organization, if the moratorium expires and first come, first serve and we don't have the rules that strike that kind of responsible approach we've been talking about here today, basically you can go your own way with respect to drilling in the Western Gap.

I think that's something we want to avoid. So I intend to work very closely with you and our committee. I think we got on the record what we needed to today.

I particularly wanted to close and let you all at least have the last word. But January 17th is coming up here. To in effect say, alright, we're not going to act. It's going to be open season there.

First come, first serve. That would not be in the interest of the American people.

So last word from my friend, Senator Murkowski.

Senator MURKOWSKI. I like having the last word. What I will remind our colleagues is that once again while things seem to be stalled out in other parts of this building, as a committee, we're trying to move through some good stuff. Last week while all eyes were focused upon a few key individuals and quite honestly we weren't getting a lot of governing done, you and I and our very able staffs worked with our colleagues on the House side to move through the Helium bill.

There wasn't front page news that I could find about it and that was just fine because, quite honestly, we got an important provision moved through both bodies and around the road blocks and to the President for his signature. We're just kind of quietly doing our work here. I think with the frustration that the public feels right now about what is happening in the Congress or perhaps the lack of anything happening in the Congress right now as they see their government shutting down.

I think it's important to know that on this first morning of the government shut down we're talking about how we, as a Nation, move forward toward energy independence, North American energy independence, energy security, working to make sure that we've got environmental frameworks in place, safety frameworks in place. I just appreciate the fact that we're continuing to do what I think people sent us to do which is get to work.

So I appreciate your leadership here this morning. Appreciate those of you that took the time to be with us and to speak up on what I think is a pretty important issue for our country.

So, thank you.

[Whereupon, at 11:10 a.m., the hearing was adjourned.]

APPENDIX

RESPONSES TO ADDITIONAL QUESTIONS

RESPONSES OF CARLOS PASCUAL TO QUESTIONS FROM SENATOR JOHNSON

Question 1. I am a strong supporter of section 1504 of the Dodd-Frank legislation requiring expanded transparency for extractive industries, and oppose the House attempt to incorporate an exemption into legislation on this agreement. In your view, is the agreement, as it was negotiated, implementable—where U.S. companies can participate in these transboundary projects—without undermining Section 1504, as the provision in H.R. 1613 has sought to do?

Answer. The Department of State strongly supports Dodd-Frank Section 1504, which set an important new standard for transparency in the extractive industries. As I noted in my testimony, we look forward to working with the Congress to enact implementing legislation that would focus on the U.S.-Mexico Transboundary Agreement, without the inclusion of extraneous and unnecessary provisions such as those relating to Dodd-Frank Section 1504. Such inclusions would directly and negatively affect U.S. efforts to increase transparency and accountability. The provisions are unnecessary and unrelated to implementing the U.S.-Mexico Transboundary Hydrocarbon Agreement and seriously detract from the bill.

Question 2. The Mexican government has indicated its intent to implement the Extractive Industries Transparency Initiative (EITI) and is a founding member of the Open Government Partnership with the United States. Has the State Department or the U.S. Embassy in Mexico received any indication that the Mexican government is preparing legislation to prevent disclosure in transboundary waters?

Answer. We are not aware of any plans by the Government of Mexico to introduce legislation preventing disclosure of payments for commercial development of oil, gas, or minerals in transboundary waters. We welcome the Government of Mexico's strong engagement on the Open Government Partnership (OGP) and we look forward to their implementation of the EITI. The United States also strongly supports the EITI by participating actively on its international governing board, funding technical assistance, and promoting the initiative in bilateral discussions as well as multilateral groups such as the G8 and G20. The State Department collaborates closely with colleagues at the U.S. Department of the Interior as they work with civil society, industry, and Federal and state government representatives toward implementing the EITI domestically in the United States, which is one of our commitments in the U.S. Open Government Partnership National Action Plan.

RESPONSE OF CARLOS PASCUAL TO QUESTION FROM SENATOR SCHATZ

Question 1. Ambassador Pascual, I wonder if you could discuss the benefits of reporting requirements under Section 1504 of the Dodd-Frank Act, the initiatives in place at the State Department, and how the exemption in the House bill would affect your agency's efforts at achieving transparency.

Answer. The U.S. Department of State strongly supports Dodd-Frank Section 1504, which sets an important new standard for transparency in the extractive industries. As I noted in my testimony, we look forward to working with the Congress to enact implementing legislation that would focus on the U.S.-Mexico Transboundary Agreement, without the inclusion of extraneous provisions such as those relating to Dodd-Frank Section 1504. Not only are the provisions unnecessary and unrelated to implementing the U.S.-Mexico Transboundary Hydrocarbon Agreement; they would directly and negatively affect U.S. efforts to increase transparency and accountability in the extractives sector globally. Dodd-Frank Section 1504 set a new global standard for revenue transparency, one that is being emulated by others. Since the provision's passage into law in the United States, the European Union adopted similar rules and Canada is working actively to do so. This year, the G-8 Leaders encouraged other countries that host major multinational or state-owned enterprises that invest abroad to implement equivalent mandatory reporting rules. The addition of exemptions to Dodd-Frank Section 1504 as in H.R. 1613 would undermine United States and international efforts to arrive at clear and consistent reporting requirements across jurisdictions that would minimize duplicate reporting burdens, and ensure this reporting is complete.

The extractive sectors are notoriously difficult for countries to manage effectively and transparently. While these resources are key to the global economy and can be a tremendous asset for a country's economic growth, too often countries have been unable to manage the development of these resources effectively, with the result that the returns on this wealth are not leveraged into sustained economic growth. The Department supports transparency in the payments that extractive companies make to governments as a key component of a broader strategy to support effective and accountable government management of the extractive sectors. The company reporting requirements contained in Dodd-Frank Section 1504 complement voluntary initiatives like the Extractive Industries Transparency Initiative (EITI) by giving people in countries around the world the information they need to hold their own governments accountable.

○